Drawing with Shapes Is Fun!

DRAWING A TURTLE WITH HALF CIRCLES

AVERY ADAMS

PowerKiDS press
New York

Published in 2019 by The Rosen Publishing Group, Inc.
29 East 21st Street, New York, NY 10010

First Edition

Editor: Greg Roza
Book Design: Reann Nye

Photo Credits: Cover, 1–22 (background) piotr_pabijan/Shutterstock.com; cover, 1–22 (markers) Photo Melon/Shutterstock.com; pp. 5, 24 Mariyana M/Shutterstock.com.

Cataloging-in-Publication Data

Names: Adams, Avery.
Title: Drawing a turtle with half circles / Avery Adams.
Description: New York : PowerKids Press, 2019. | Series: Drawing with shapes is fun! | Includes index.
Identifiers: LCCN ISBN 9781538331248 (pbk.) | ISBN 9781538331231 (library bound) | ISBN 9781538331255 (6 pack)
Subjects: LCSH: Turtles in art–Juvenile literature. | Circle in art–Juvenile literature. | Drawing–Technique–Juvenile literature.
Classification: LCC NC655.A325 2019 | DDC 743.6'792–dc23

Manufactured in the United States of America

CPSIA Compliance Information: Batch #CS18PK: For Further Information contact Rosen Publishing, New York, New York at 1-800-237-9932

CONTENTS

Turtles stay warm by sitting in the sun. Let's draw a turtle!

Draw a yellow half circle for the **shell** of your turtle.

Draw a small pink half circle for the tail of your turtle.

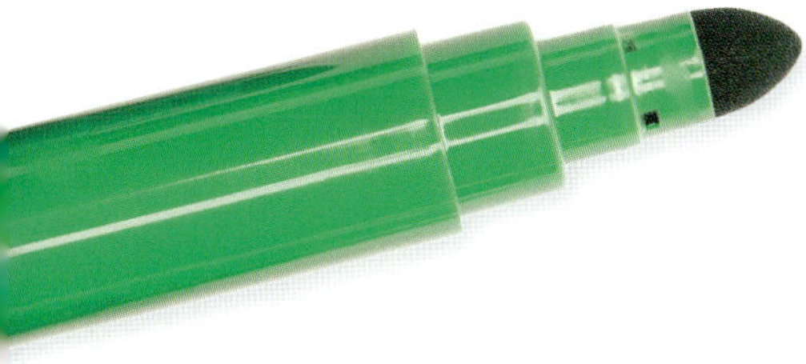

Draw a green half circle for the **head** of your turtle.

Draw a purple half circle for the back **foot** of your turtle.

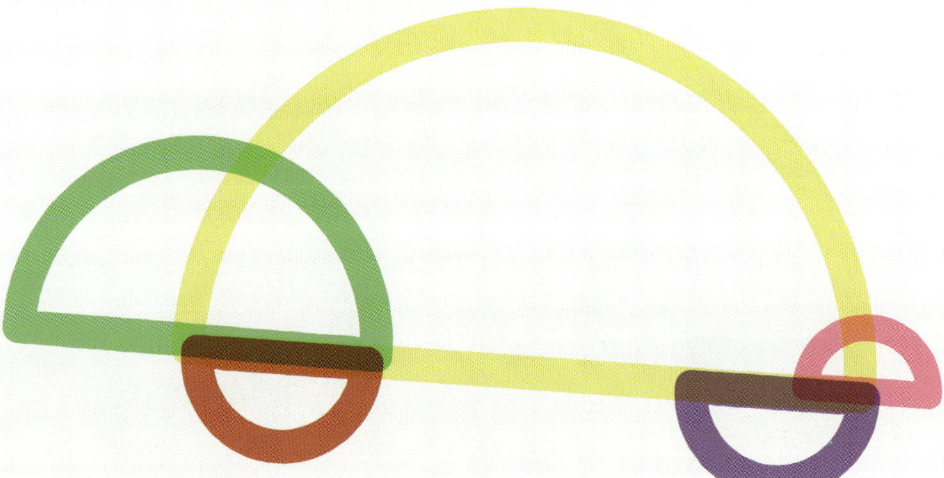

Draw a red half circle for the front foot of your turtle.

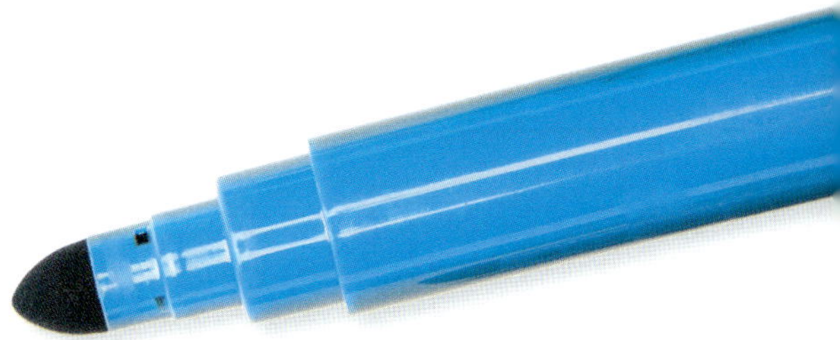

Draw a blue half circle to make an eye for your turtle.

Draw five orange half circles on the shell of your turtle.

Add a black half circle to the eye of your turtle.

Color in your turtle. Nice work!

WORDS TO KNOW

foot

head

shell

INDEX

WEBSITES

Due to the changing nature of Internet links, PowerKids Press has developed an online list of websites related to the subject of this book. This site is updated regularly. Please use this link to access the list: www.powerkidslinks.com/dws/turt